HEALING TESTIMONY OF DAVID ANTONY CAMPBELL

1st Printing 2021 by Websity Limited, Nottingham, United Kingdom

Find out more about David Antony Campbell at: David Kindle Ministry

Email: davekind1999@gmail.com

Website: www.davidkindle.co.uk

Facebook: David Campbell

Twitter: @DavidKindleMinistry

ISBN: 978-1-8384558-0-4

CW00550664

PREFACE

I have known Evangelist David Campbell and his family for over twenty years and have the pleasure to serve as his Pastor. I have seen some of his great struggles and can confirm his testimony of God's unconditional love, grace and mercy. This book is a great and powerful testimony to God's unreserved love and healing that all can receive. I believe this book will deliver people and give them hope and faith in God. I am pleased to read this book and see his journey with God. I also saw the demonstration of His divine healing that is given to all through His suffering, crucifixion and resurrection in David's life. Apostle Paul states in Philippians 1 verse 21,

"*For me to live is Christ and to die is gain*" and in Romans 8 verse 18, "*I resolved that our present sufferings are not to be compared to the glory that will be revealed in us*". God bless you and continue to fight the good fight of faith. Amen.

Dr Bishop Joan Richards.
Apostle of Elohim Ministries.

DEDICATION

This book is dedicated to my mother, the late Mrs. Doren Campbell, for her love, care and exemplary Christian lifestyle which she demonstrated in practical terms during her lifetime. She taught me how to trust God during the difficult times and how to be a cheerful giver.

The testimony shared in this book is a product of the moral lessons she impacted to me to be grateful to God always for every victory attained over the battles of life. I am forever grateful to God who has given me the privilege to be your son. I love you mummy. Sleep on.

TABLE OF CONTENT

INTRODUCTION

Praise the Lord! David Anthony Campbell is my name. I am popularly known as David Kindle. I was born in Nottingham, United Kingdom. I am so delighted to write this book to testify to the healing power of God in my life. I was in despair of sickness and lost hope of survival. The Consultant in the Queen's Medical Centre in Nottingham gave me few weeks to live when he discovered that my kidneys had failed. But God had mercy on me, delivered me from the power of death and divinely healed me and got my kidneys functioning again. This book is a great testimony of God's unconditional love for me through Christ's suffering, crucifixion and resurrection.

"But he was wounded for our transgressions, he was bruised for our iniquities: the chastisement of our peace was upon him; and with his stripe we are healed." Isaiah 53:5.

David praising God after he came out of the hospital

In my early life, I used to be a reggae musician but, by divine providence, God made me a gospel singer in 1982 before I became an Evangelist in 2007 through the gospel songs. Maintaining my religious connection to God and other Christians has been very important thing to me since I knew the Lord Jesus as my personal Lord and saviour in 1980.

About my far reaching sickness, according to the Consultant, the complexities of the illness started unawares in 2004 (about sixteen year ago) when I was initially diagnosed of type II diabetes Mellitus before the full diagnosis of 2012 that so traumatized me. Further to this, I suffered brain injury which I sustained from the road accident, physical attacks and stroke. Eventually, I also had cardiac failures,

Oedema, kidney failure, lung failure, flu, skin rashes, swollen stomach and legs. Friends, family members and many church members rallied around me during this period. When the Consultant declared I had but a few weeks to live, everyone lost hope. I lost hope in myself too. I was expecting my last breath on the surface of the earth. The experience of one's knowledge of end of life was an horrible one. The Consultant confirmed my liver was working at two percent function, my lungs were at two percent, my kidneys had stopped working totally and the Consultant stopped my medication because there was no hope of survival. On this note, I was discharged from the hospital without medication.

My situation was narrated to Pastor Castro Banefe of Regenerated Church of God. The church members and the pastor prayed fervently for a healing miracle to happen in my life and God honoured their prayers. I told the story to other pastors and saints in Nottingham too. They all prayed for me and God honoured their prayers. Praise God! While I was expecting my last breath, suddenly my liver, lungs, heart and kidneys started picking up and then gradually improved. Immediately the Consultant noticed this when I went back to the Queen's Medical Centre in Nottingham, my medication was restored and administered. At that time I could not work, I was very heavy and bloated, I started with limited mobility and very gradually improved. Glory be to God. Now I can go to the church and access the community and city centre at will with the support of personal carers. God answered the prayers of brethren. God had mercy on me, even at the point when I could not open my mouth to pray.

"O give thanks unto the LORD; for he is good: for his mercy endures forever. O give thanks unto the God of gods: for his mercy endures forever. O give thanks to the Lord of lords: for his mercy endures forever. To him who alone doeth great wonders: for his mercy endures forever." Psalm 136:1 – 4.

"Bless the LORD, O my soul: and all that is within me, bless his holy name. Bless the LORD, O my soul, and forget not all his benefits: Who forgives all thin iniquities; who heals all thy diseases; Who redeems thy life from destruction; who crowns thee with loving-kindness and tender mercies; Who satisfies thy mouth with good things; so that thy youth is renewed like the eagle's." Psalm 103:1 – 5.

My motivation for this book is God Who had proven wrong the Consultant who said I had a few weeks to live in 2018, but I have outlived that. God further saved someone who was about to commit suicide due to what he had been through, who attended the Prophet Uebert Angel Church in Birmingham for the first time where he heard me sharing my testimonies in the church. He shed tears and came to find out from me if my testimonies were true. A life was saved that day. Glory be to God! Based on all these things, I have decided to put the story of my testimonies in a moderately sized book titled "The Healing Testimony of David A. Campbell" to encourage people, save many lives and help spread the gospel of Jesus Christ.

This book comprises six short chapters. Each chapter is unique. Chapter one is about my background, early life, family life and ministerial life. Chapter two is about how my sickness started. Chapter three is the episode of my bitter experience during the sickness. Chapter four is the great revelation of Christ as the Mighty Healer and sundry testimonies from various believers and pastors about me. Chapter five is about the details of divine healing and health as encouragement to the sick. Finally, the last chapter is the conclusion and appreciation to the individuals, family members and churches who stood by me during my sickness.

David in Nottingham city

CHAPTER ONE
MY EARLY LIFE AND BACKGROUND

This chapter gives the details of my background. As earlier mentioned in my introduction, I was born into the family of Mr. Johney Campbell and Mrs. Doreen Campbell. They were laid to rest a few years ago. May their souls rest in perfect peace. I was born in Nottingham, England. I attended my primary and high school in Nottingham. I grew up under the influence of my mother who was a loving and caring woman during her lifetime. My parents are Jamaica–British. I speak both Jamaican and English languages fluently.

I attended Mount Zion Apostolic Church in Nottingham during my childhood with my late grandmother Jones and family. The memory of Christian lessons in Mount Zion Apostolic Church is always fresh in me. It's a loving and caring church where I did my water baptism in 1980.

Mount Zion Apostolic Church
where I grew up

I am now a family man and blessed with children. All my children are grown up. I brought them up in God's way. Three are already married with children, my grandkids. I lived most of my life for volunteer works in Nottingham, such as Sickle Cell Fund Raising, Council Research and Charity Supports. I am passionate about helping the needy and getting involved in charity works. I have worked as a bouncer and Bus Station cleaner before I retired into the music industry. I enjoyed listening to music, most especially gospel songs and reggae music. I started singing when I was fourteen years old. I discovered in 1982 that I could do better if I transferred my music talent fully to gospel songs, which I did, although whenever I sang my reggae music, it was always full of biblical inspirations and words of love. Sometimes, I did quote some Bible verses in my reggae music and sometimes channelled it towards praising God, rapping the victory of God over Satan, preaching the gospel of Jesus and many others.

David Campbell performing live on the stage in Nigeria

In 2007, I became an ordained Evangelist at the "Strong Tower Church of Holy Spirit" in Nigeria. It was a glorious experience in my life. Since my ordination, the inspiration of God in the gospel songs has ever been multiplying within my life. I produced my first music album entitled, "My God is real" in 2007.

I have ministered in song at many churches in England, places like Nottingham, Leicester, Manchester, Birmingham and London. I have travelled to Africa (Nigeria) to minister in gospel songs.

My first album titled: *My God is real*

I love the Lord and have been a Christian all through my life. I am very religious and consecration towards God has been my priority. I am not attached to a particular church in Nottingham, but I attend different churches every Sunday to offer myself as a living sacrifice. I am a singer and man of prayers. I pray a lot. Two of my favourite songs are:

1. *"There are some places, I may not go;*
There are some things, I may not know;
But this one thing, I am sure;
My God is real;
For I can feel it, deep in the my soul;

My God is real, deep in my soul;
His love for me is more precious more than Gold;
If not for Him who saved my soul;
My God is real;
For I can feel it, deep in the my soul".

2. *"I need Thee, oh, I need Thee;*
Every hour I need Thee;
Oh, bless me now, my Savior!
I come to Thee".

My background was full of challenges as I grew up with a single mother. I was faced with enormous physical and spiritual attacks. My life was full of struggles and travails. My problems got worse when I was diagnosed. This traumatized me further. I was almost dead at one point, but God brought me back to life. For more than seven years, I have been reliant on the support of personal carers who got me back into the community. I received support to do things I once enjoyed and could do on my own. I required support to manage essential aids to daily living (ADL) including personal care, nutritional health, maintaining a habitable home, shopping at the city centre and accessing essential community services. Sometimes I went out on my scooter to access the community. At some points, it was difficult to maintain a meaningful relationship with people whenever I was upset. This I have overcome since I started regaining my perfect health.

"Man that is born of a woman is of few days and full of trouble. He comes forth like a flower and is cut down: he flees also as a shadow and continues not." Job 14:1-2.

Currently, I have reasons to praise God. I can do many things now with little support from my carers. Jesus visited me. My health is improving, my distended body is gradually returning to normal body size. My dead lungs, liver, heart and kidneys are now functioning again. My friends and family are glad to see what God is doing in my life. I am happy now, Praise God!

18

CHAPTER TWO

BEGINNING OF MY SICKNESS

This chapter describes how my sickness started and the enormous health challenges I encountered in life. In my early twenties, I sustained a brain injuiry due to the skull fracture I had when I was hit on the head with hammer and at other times stabbed three times when I was working as a night security guard in Nottingham. I was later diagnosed with amnesia when I started showing the symptoms because I was unable to form new memories, with difficulty in recalling facts, events, places and specific details both at work and home. This situation was managed for several years before I eventually became very sick.

The complexities of my health issues and sickness began unawares in 2004 according to the Consultant. I was worried when I started feeling weak on a daily basis. On 22 September 2004, I was diagnosed with type II diabetes Mellitus in Queen's Medical Centre in Nottingham. On 6 November 2004, I was again diagnosed with hyperlipidaemia in same hospital and this sickness continued until 2012. Everything got complicated when I was further diagnosed with heart failure in 2012. At this point. I enquired from the doctor the likely cause of my illness. I also visited a Cardiology Consultant who commented 'idiopathic', which means no distinct cause was found. This is usually because investigations were either normal or incomplete. As an estimate, this makes up about fifteen percent (15%) of heart failure cases.

In June 2012, I came under the care of another Cardiology Consultant following a referral to the Heart Failure Nurse Specialist (HENS) who offered a coronary angiography to investigate the aetiology of my heart failure. I was admitted by emergency in September 2012, where I was transferred for angiography that revealed no significant coronary disease in keeping with the diagnosis of dilated cardiomyopathy before I was discharged. The usual practice is that the nurses or staff would refer a patient with heart failure to the Community Heart Failure Team (CHFT) which did occur in my case. I was re-admitted for heart failure management at the request of my daughter. It was later that the Queen's Medical Centre asked the Primary Care Heart Failure Specialist (PCHFS) to review me in the community. I went back to the Queen's Medical Centre in April 2013 where I was transferred from one ward to another. I was in the hospital for about six mouths. Towards the end of the six months, the Nottingham City Council had approved regular carers for me. My personal carers were with me on a shift arrangement to support me.

It was documented on 30 September 2013 that a Consultant was called to speak to my son regarding my discharge. The Consultant explained to him about the treatments I had received while in the hospital and that I was fit for discharge, but my son did not subscribe to my discharge and became angry with the Consultant. The National Health Scheme (NHS) team explained to him their value and behaviour policy which applies to all staff, patients and visitors. This matter escalated and came to the attention of the Cardiology Registrar who suggested it was not appropriate or safe to discharge me until further general practitioner (GP) and social services documentation had taken place. I later assured the Consultant that I would be fine on my discharge since I had personal carers with me.

In July 2016, I was knocked down by a car in Saint Ann's in Nottingham. I was on the ground writhing in pain as a result of the collision with the car. At the scene of the accident were police officers who did not interview me or show concern for my situation but told me in my state of agony that I was guilty of the collision.

Furthermore, on 15 December 2018, I had a tram accident that almost claimed my life. The tram driver applied the brake suddenly to avoid collision with a van along Radford Road. This led to about six people falling on me. I fell from my scooter. My head banged on the floor. I suffered stomach and leg injuries. It was a horrible experience in my life. The tram accident is still under investigation at the time of writing this book. I was referred to an independent consultant who would make a medical report to establish the extent of my sustained injuries during the accident and whether I had ongoing symptoms and to provide a prognosis.

My illness was far reaching, including brain injury, stroke, cardiac failure, type II diabetes mellitus, oedema, kidney failure, swollen body, dead body skin, terrible itchiness, to name but a few. My daughter later joined the league of my personal carers. My problem worsened when she went to live in Jamaica, though she was contacted and returned to the UK in the hospital to cater for me. I have been through a lot in my life. It affected me mentally, psychologically, emotionally and spiritually. Everyone lost hope in my survival when my heart, liver and kidneys were working at two percent (2%), but God intervened in my situation, brought me back to life and made all my internal organs start functioning again. I am grateful to God!

CHAPTER THREE
MY BITTER EXPERIENCES DURING THE SICKNESS

In this chapter I would like to talk about my unpalatable experiences during the illness.

"The sorrow of death compassed me and the pains of hell get hold upon me; I found trouble and sorrow." Psalms 116: 3.

The bitter experience started immediately I was diagnosed with cardiac failure which traumatised me. I could neither walk fast nor cover a long distance again, I could not do the things that I once enjoyed doing myself. I could not get back to the community without support because I could forget the way due to my partial memory loss. My gospel music ministry went down, no more church singing, no more street singing at the city centre, no more cooking for myself. It was a devastating experience. I was living completely on the mercies of my personal carers and family members.

Due to the shortness of my breath at night and sleep apnoea, I always use a Continuous Positive Airway Pressure (CPAP) machine at night. I had cardiac failure staff to support me with putting on the mask at night and monitoring throughout the night. The cardiac failure staff would ensure that the mask did not get dislodged but in the event that it did, it would be replaced. With the CPAP machine,

I get enough oxygen throughout the night. As I said earlier, I also required support to manage essential Activities of Daily Living (ADL) such as personal care, cleaning of the house, writing and reading of mails. My day support staff would give me personal care and get me dressed for the day. The day support staff prepare my meals and administer my medication all through the week.

Another bitter experience was the difficulties in defecation. My significant chronic medical conditions compromised my ability to perform excretion appropriately. I was also obese with increased osteoarthritis in my hands. The shower, toilet and bidet which were not in proximity for me to be able to care for myself compounded my problems. The excretion difficulty continued to compromise the care I received which left me extremely vulnerable to significant medical complications. With this, an urgent assessment was recommended of my house. The recommendation made as a result of the assessment led to relief when a two-bedroom bungalow was allocated to me by Nottingham Council in Beechdale.

The most painful experience during the sickness was when I was knocked down by a driver in Saint Ann's. The police's resolution about the incident was unsatisfactory to me. The police insisted I was guilty and they refused to carry out investigations into the accident. The police did not provide CCTV evidence. Meanwhile I hired a solicitor who was able to obtain the CCTV evidence from another source to support my case with the insurance company of the driver. I really went through agony and pains because of the accident. The shock from the accident led to brain injuries and partial memory loss. Sometimes, I wandered around the community, forgetting the road to my house due to the partial memory loss. I could only access the community with the aid of a scooter and with a personal carer beside me. It was a terrible experience of travail of life for me.

Finally, I became disabled with severely restricted mobility. I was bloated (I became excessively overweight) and could only walk slowly and for a short distance within the house. These and many other terrible experiences befell me during my sickness.

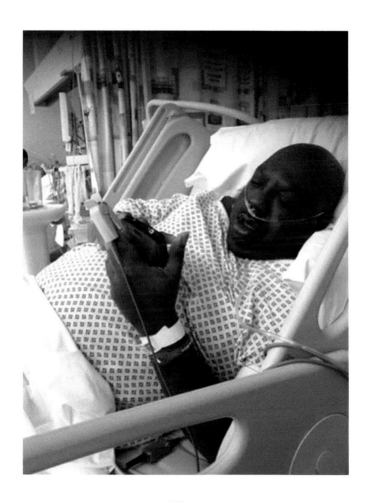

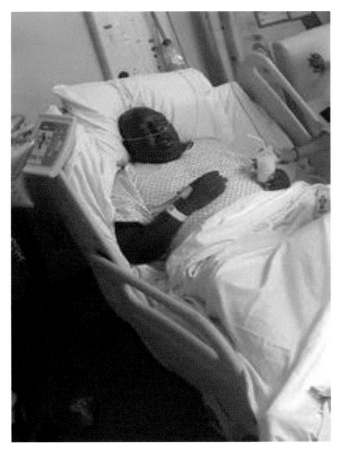

David campbell in hospital bed

CHAPTER FOUR

CHRIST, THE MIGHTY HEALER

At this point, I would like to convince you that God is real. His mercy is the reason for my healing and why I am alive alive today.

"He loves me, I cannot say why...
He loves me, I cannot say why...
On Calvary tree, He died for me
He loves me, I cannot say why".

During the sickness, I enjoyed the visitations, care and prayers of pastors and church members from different churches in Nottingham. They all gave me both physical and spiritual support. Most especially, the pastor and members of the Regenerated

Church of God in Nottingham prayed tirelessly for me. Sometimes, they would manage to get me to the church auditorium, where they would pray and anoint me in accordance with the scriptures.

"Is any sick among you? Let him call for the elders of the church, and let them pray over him, anointing him with oil in the name of the Lord. And the prayer of faith shall save the sick and the Lord shall raise him up; and if he has committed sins, they shall be forgiven him." James 2:14-15.

God answered the prayers of His children. He had mercy on me. He remembered my labours of love and healed all my sicknesses.

"Many are the afflictions of the righteous; but the Lord delivers him out of them all." Psalm 34:17.

As an Evangelist, I have been to many churches in England to minister without charging money. God rewarded me in an immense way by healing me when I did not even have a little strength to pray, but the people of God rose to my support by praying for me. I am grateful to God. I am a living testimony to the glory of God. The Consultant who declared me 'the end of life patient' saw me a few months later. He tagged me "a man with nine lives" and was amazed that I was still alive. I was placed on an end of life and palliative care plan, but today I am still living by the grace of God. He has laid His hand of healing upon me. My health is now steadily improving.

The following testimonies are the eyewitness accounts of: one of my pastors; a friend and a church member about the healing power of Jesus Christ in my life.

My Pastor's testimony:

"My name is Pastor Castro Banefe. I am by the grace of God the founder and Senior Pastor of the Regenerated Church of God currently located on 18A Peveril Street, NG7 4AH, Nottingham. I have known Evangelist David Campbell since 2016 and ever since then we have been relating as brethren. In the month of May 2018, David invited me to his house

and disclosed his health issues to me. According to him, the Consultant told him and his family members about his health conditions that he was having multiple organ failure (kidney, liver and lung) which would shortly result in his death. On the basis of this, he was given but a few weeks to live. According to him, his body was no longer responding to medical treatment and this resulted in the withdrawal of his medication.

I encouraged Evangelist David that if he had faith in God and His word, he would live and not die according to Psalm 118:17. On that very day, I prayed with him and invited him to Church the next Sunday. David could not lift himself up to enter the church bus, but he was supported by some brethren. He also needed support to climb the stairs into the church auditorium (rails were put in place immediately to ease mobility for him). David could not walk at all even with his walking stick. At the Regenerated Church of God, I invited the choir team to be praising and giving thanks to God while I led prayers for David according to the following scriptures: Acts 12:5, Ezekiel 37: 4-14. Furthermore, David was anointed in the church with the anointing oil. Immediately after the prayers, we started seeing changes in his mobility, he could do better than when we brought him in. Prophesy and word of knowledge came out to David for his health and for the regaining of his strength. Since then David continued to worship with us at the Regenerated Church of God."

39

Pastor Castro F. E. Banefe, Senior Pastor, Regenerated Church of God.

My friend's testimony:

"I am Pele Liburd. By the grace of God, I am born again and a practising Christian. I have known David over the years (more than 10 years precisely) and recently met him again when I heard that he was very sick and close to death. As an eyewitness, I have seen the hand of the Lord Jesus Christ in his life, which revived him and restored his health. David loves to minister in gospel songs. May the good Lord continue to bless him in his endeavours."
Pele Liburd (GEM ministry),
p.liburd@hotmail.com

Another friend's testimony:

"My name is C. James. David Campbell has been my friend for many years. He has always been kind and thoughtful. Early this year I was sad to hear of his sickness. I went to visit him at his home and I was shocked to see his condition. It seemed that he was on a pathway to palliative care. He declined so quickly. The next I heard he was in Queen's Medical Centre in Nottingham. I decided to be brave, to go and visit, but I was shocked to be told he had only few weeks to live. After he returned home under a team of carers, I noticed he started experiencing faith in God. We prayed and sang almost daily over the phone. He started to worship God, truly believing in His healing. David seems to be much better

41

and can truly and sincerely say he has been blessed. Thank God for David Campbell's blessing."

Mrs. C. James.
Jamescheryl350@outlook.com

Eye witness testimony

My name is Emelda. I live in Nottingham. I am a member of UCKG HelpCentre (Charity organization in Nottingham). I know David for a long time. For the past three years, he wasn't very well in a way he was in the wheel chair. He was very polly. When I met him in the bus, Jesus ministered to my spirit to invite him to one of our programs. I invited him and he did come when there was an event. I was very happy for that one.

On 2 April 2021, I met him again at the Nottingham city centre with his personal carer. I was amazed to see him still alive. Oh my God! He was in good health. One thing about this is only God's power from above can do this. I couldn't believe how David was able to survive and recover from that situation because he was at the verge of death. I was very happy to say this testimony on a video clip with David at the Nottingham city centre. This is a big testimony. Thank you Jesus for the healing testimony of David Campbell.

Emelda.

Nottingham.

David Campbell in one of his stage performances

44

CHAPTER FIVE

DIVINE HEALING AND HEALTH

In this chapter, the scriptural details of divine healing and health are given. The Christian perspectives and what are expected of all believers to enjoy the divine healing and health are elaborated.

Divine healing and health have been viewed from different angles by believers of different ages. This has always been as a result of man's perception of the limit of God's power, mercy and love. However, from time immemorial, believers have always been receivers while sceptics have received nothing. Similarly, if we believe today, all divine blessings, including healing and health, can be ours.

45

"According as his divine power hath given unto us all things that pertain unto life and godliness, through the knowledge of him that hath called us to glory and virtue." 2 Peter 1:3.

A survey of the length and breadth of the history of God's dealings with man reveals that healing is God's will. God is a good God and it is His will that His children live in good health as well as enjoy divine healing throughout their days on earth. This thought is unequivocally stated by John the beloved in his epistle.

"Beloved, I wish above all things that thou may prosper and be in health, even as thy soul prospers." 3 John: 2.

It is not the will of God that any of His children should remain in sickness, oppression or disease. There are one hundred and forty-five occurrences of the words heal, healed, healer, heals, healing, healings and health in the Bible, which is an indication of the divine plan concerning our healing and health. Since Old Testament days, healing has always been an integral part of God's covenant with His people. God has always included it as a part of His blessings upon those who are obedient to His word.

Healing was easy in the Old Testament, but it is even much easier in the New Testament. This is because God had revealed Himself as *the God that heals*. It was so easy that Naaman almost lost the opportunity of being

47

healed. He did not expect getting healed to be so easy. He was told by Prophet Elisha just to go to Jordan, dip himself seven times into the water and he would be healed. That was not to take much time. As he went and dipped himself in the water *"according to the saying of the man of God"* he came out clean. The instruction was simple, but his healing was complete. He was healed, not by the river Jordan, but by the power and authority in the Word of God through His ordained servant. This story is found in 2King 5: 1–27. Healing and obedience to the instructions of God and His ordained servants are inseparable. While venomous snakes were biting the children of Israel and many of them were dying, they were told to obey a simple instruction: look up and be healed. This story is found in Number 21: 1–9. This same principle applies also in the New Testament. We are to look up to Jesus Christ who died on the cross. Hannah, who because of her barrenness was in bitterness of soul, had her situation changed for life as a result of just an eighteen-word pronouncement of Eli the man of God.

"Then Eli answered and said, go in peace: and the God of Israel grant you your petition that you have asked of him." 1 Samuel 1:17.

It was that simple. If you are barren, the Lord can heal and make you fruitful, if you can believe the words of God and stop fretting yourself. During His earthly ministry, Jesus healed people in cities and villages of His day. As there were no hospitals as we have them today, they lived in primitive conditions and there were a lot of sicknesses and diseases among the people. In His characteristic lifestyle, Jesus would teach in the synagogue, preach the kingdom of God and heal those who were sick among them. This was His three-piece method: teaching, preaching and healing. As the people came to listen to His teachings and preaching, they applied what they were taught to their lives and it generated faith in them and they were healed.

A clear understanding of what the Bible teaches about healing and health ensures a continuous state of soundness for the believers. Healing and health belong to the children of God. A careful study of God's word deepens the truth in the believer's heart and helps him to apply it to his life. This in turn will generate and increase faith in his heart.

"So then faith comes by hearing, and hearing by the word of God." Roman 10:17.

Healing is not needed in heaven, as there is no sickness there. It is for God's children on earth and they should expect to be healed any time they are sick. Just as when children are hungry, parents always make bread available. Also whenever a child of God is sick, God always makes healing available. If you are sick, God can heal you. Every morning, children ask bread of their parents without doubting. They believe that their parents can provide for them, so they are not afraid. Believers are to come to God for healing with that same confidence. They should realize that healing is their bread and it is available for them. The healing and health that unbelievers enjoy are crumbs that fall from the children's bread. It is worthwhile remembering that after Jesus had fed the five thousand people, there were still twelve baskets remaining. For every crumb of healing and health that unbelievers enjoy from God, there is abundant provision for His children to enjoy. However, believers should also bear in mind that there are others that are sick who need healing. By praying for those who are sick, believers can share their health with them.

"And these signs shall follow them that believe; In my name shall they cast out devils; they shall speak with new tongues; They shall take up serpents; and if they drink any deadly thing, it shall not hurt them; they shall lay hands on the sick, and they shall recover." Mark 16: 17-18.

This healing bread should be shared with one another. The believer does not rest his hope only on medical science for his healing and health. He also trusts God for perfect health from day to day. When he is sick, he depends on the armour of prayer and faith. However, it is not a sin to receive help from the practice of medicine that has nothing to do with invocation of evil powers. Besides, certain cases like child delivery, caesarean section, orthopedic surgery and other therapies require the skill of trained medical personnel in hospitals, maternities and clinics. We should afford ourselves of all God-provided opportunities for health and longevity. God has made every provision for our healing and health. And we should live daily in the realization of His provisions. With all the provisions that God has made for believers to enjoy healing and health, it is still necessary for man to adequately look after himself. This is the role he must play if he is to continue to enjoy good health. He should, as a matter of duty, ensure that his nutritional habit is proper and his diet balanced. He should also maintain good personal hygiene and pay attention to environmental cleanliness, appropriate physical exercise, and total avoidance of harmful habits that can damage his health. The correct intake of fruit, fibre and other nutritious foods will promote good health while wrong feeding such as the intake of junk foods only clog up the system without commensurate nutritional values. The good thing about our heavenly Father is that He has made these things available for mankind. Fruit and vegetables are not only available all year round but are also affordable to as many as are willing to utilize them, so that there is no room for excuses. If the money wasted on junk foods is thoughtfully expended on what will build up body immunity against illness, we will be saving our family and the church the agony of running from one hospital to another. Let us be wise.

Sin and sickness are close pals, so are holiness and health. Without doubt, God has an unfailing healing and health plan for mankind but there are millions of people who - by virtue of the fact that they have not come into covenant relationship with God - do not know the blessedness of enjoying these provisions.

A close look at biblical history shows that people who obey God are made and kept healthy by Him. The contrary goes for children of disobedience. Theirs is a life of turmoil, pestilence and disease. Abraham, Moses, Joshua, David, Jesus Christ, Peter and John are names that do not go hand in hand with sickness. Biblical records of sickness often go with such names as Abimelech, Manasseh, Naaman and Elymas the sorcerer, to name but a few. Hard-hearted Egyptians had a good toll of plagues and pestilence, while the children of Israel had divine prosperity and health according to God's promise.

Sometimes, sickness came as a result of the curse of the law for disobedience to God's command, though this curse may be in form of other suffering in some cases. On the contrary, God entrenched healing as an integral part of what Jesus procured for us on the cross of Calvary.

"Christ has redeemed us from the curse of the law, being made a curse for us." Galatians 3:13a.

Man may be lost in sin. But Jesus is waiting to save and to change him. All one needs to do is to take the initiative and come to the Lord and be saved. He forgives sin and saves sinners. He changes sinners and gives them power to live as sons of God. He restores the invalid to health and strength. He cures the incurable and delivers the oppressed.

There is no doubt whatsoever as to the power and willingness of God to heal all who are sick and turn to Him for help. The cases of Abimelech, Miriam, Naaman and many others are testimonies of God's willingness to "heal the sick" when they called upon Him with simple faith. It was a common phenomenon with Israel of old that diseases and evil characterized rebellious times but after repentance, obedient times became healthy times! It is clear from God's Word that all can be healed and kept healthy on a daily basis. Diligent meditation on God's Word will assure our heart of the possibility of sound health all the days of our life. God's Word is a word of power and has an innate potency for the miraculous.

"For I am not ashamed of the gospel of Christ: for it is the power of God unto salvation to

everyone that believes; to the Jew first, and also to the Greek." Romans 1:16.

Besides, the power of God is unlimited. Generally, the Bible highlights two types of power; the dynamic power and the legal power (in Greek: "dunamis" and "exousia" respectively). The first connotes ability, energy and strength, the second, authority, right and attorney. The Father gave both to the Son. The Son has, in turn given them to the believers.

"Why should it be thought a thing incredible with you, that God should raise the dead?" Acts 26:8.

The same power that God had since eternity is still at work today for the believer. But only those who would dare believe receive. God's will is clear on healing and health: It is His will that you enjoy them. God's name, love and mercy all make us to know that we need not remain under the curse of the law again. God's revealed redemptive names are seven in number and they are:

Jehovah Shamma – *The Lord our Presence*
Jehovah Shalom – *The Lord our Peace*
Jehovah Ra-ah– *The Lord our Shepherd*
Jehovah Jireh – *The Lord our Provision*
Jehovah Nissi – *The Lord our Banner*
Jehovah Tsidkenu– *The Lord our Righteousness*
Jehovah Rapha – *The Lord our Healer*

Nothing sets forth the validity of God's willingness and ability to heal His people and keep them healthy more aptly than the last on the list of His redemptive names viz; Jehovah Rapha or Jehovah Ropheka: "I am the LORD that heals you" or "I am the LORD thy healer".

"How God anointed Jesus of Nazareth with the Holy Ghost and with power: who went about doing good and healing all that were oppressed of the devil; for God was with Him." Acts10:38.

Of course, this was to declare that healing and health are His will and to show His readiness to do His people good. Love gives to the needy and relieves suffering while mercy withholds suffering from those who rightly merit it. God is all-loving and merciful. Sicknesses and diseases are therefore definitely not from God, they are from the devil.

The Spirit of God dwells in the believer. This is the same Spirit through whose agency He made the world and everything therein at the completion of which everything was very good. It will give no credit to the Lord for the third Person in the Godhead to co-habit the same temple (our bodies) with Satan's agents such as sickness and diseases. For this cause also, the child of God can and should remain healthy.

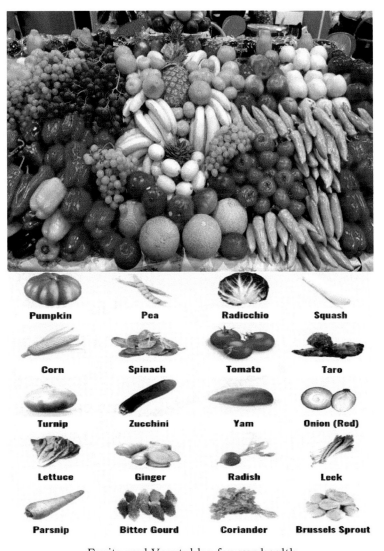

Pumpkin	Pea	Radicchio	Squash
Corn	Spinach	Tomato	Taro
Turnip	Zucchini	Yam	Onion (Red)
Lettuce	Ginger	Radish	Leek
Parsnip	Bitter Gourd	Coriander	Brussels Sprout

Fruits and Vegetables for our health

64

CHAPTER SIX

MY CONCLUSION, JOY AND CONFIDENCE IN CHRIST

I would like to conclude this book with a passionate exhortation of Apostle Paul to the Philippian brethren which was concluded with an affectionate salutation and benediction according to the Epistle to the Philippians chapter four verse one to twenty-three (Philippians 4: 1-23). The joy of the Apostle was palpable. He expressed it in the salvation of the brethren and in their gracious care for his needs. He exhorted them to "Rejoice in the Lord always..." Paul's confidence in the text was firmly based on:

(1) His hope of eternal reward.

(2) The visible evidence of genuine spiritual experiences of his fellow labourers.

(3) The ability of God to supply all the needs of His praying and faithful saints and to give them incomprehensible peace in a precarious and failing economy.

(4) The acceptability of the sacrifice of his life and ministry to God, which he recommended to the brethren as a pattern.

(5) Inner spiritual strength from Christ to serve God in all circumstances and overcome the temptations concomitant with poverty or prosperity. As an effective minister, Apostle Paul understood the importance of unity or working together to achieve a common purpose. Therefore, he enjoined the Philippians believers as follows;

"...be of the same mind in the Lord..." and *"...help those women which laboured with me in the gospel, with Clement also and with other my fellow-labourers, whose names are in the book of life."* Philippians 4:3.

He exhorted them to make the Lord the great object of their affections, bury all their petty differences and show consideration for his fellow labourers. As believers, we should support those who labour sacrificially among us and are faithful to the gospel.

"Let your moderation be known unto all men. The Lord is at hand. Be careful of nothing; but in everything by prayer and supplication with

thanksgiving let your requests be made known unto God." Philippians 4:5-6.

Again, Apostle Paul emphasized on the indispensability of a watchful, moderate, worry-free, peaceful, prayerful, thankful and godly life in everything. The Apostle admonished the Philippians not to indulge in excess of passion, dressing, eating or drinking. They were to govern their appetites and restrain their tempers so to be examples of what was proper for men in view of the expectation that the Lord would soon appear. The imminent return of Christ calls for moderation in the way believers live.

Food, clothing, shelter and safety are some of the basic concerns people worry about. Worriers think and see problems, Satan, impossibilities, impending doom, death and many others. But Paul the apostle says it is unreasonable for a child of God to get so preoccupied with challenges of life which will always be there. If anyone had any cause to worry, Paul should as he wrote the epistle from his prison ward. Despite problems and challenges, the proper conduct of anyone who believes in God is to "Be careful for nothing; but in everything by prayer and supplication with thanksgiving let your requests be made known unto God". Before and after prayer and thanksgiving, believers need to "gird up the loins of their mind…" 1 Peter 1:13, to filter out worry-induced thoughts and darts of the wicked aimed at weakening or discouraging them. The Apostle enjoined the Philippians

69

believers to program their minds with thoughts that are true, honest, just, pure, lovely, good, virtuous and praiseworthy. This means that believers are required to have the mind of Christ and walk as He also walked. To have the mind of Christ and think wholesome thoughts that translate into Christ-like conduct, the word of God must dwell richly in our heart.

"Let the word of Christ dwell in you richly in all wisdom; teaching and admonishing one another in psalms and hymns and spiritual songs, singing with grace in your hearts to the Lord." Colossians 3:16.

This way, we will be able to live impactful lives to the glory of God. Paul was a single-minded minister who did the will of God at great costs. He was a model in Christian service and did not abuse the privilege of his apostleship. He laboured more abundantly and suffered most for the gospel of Christ than all the other apostles. He toiled relentlessly to win souls and nurture them in the Lord for no pecuniary benefits. When opportunities avail itself, he would labour with his hands to provide his own physical needs. Although he had taught the truth that "...they which preach the gospel should live of the gospel". 1Corinthians 9:14, harbor no grudges for failure of some of the churches to meet his physical needs.

"I have learned, in whatsoever state I am, therewith to be contented. I know both how to be abased, and I know how to abound: everywhere and in all things, I am instructed to be full and to be hungry, to abound and to suffer need. I can do all things through Christ which strengthens me." Philippians 4:11-13.

He is not moved by lack or plenty, the generosity of the Philippians church was an encouragement to him. He said,

"...I rejoiced in the Lord greatly, that now at last your care of me has flourished again; wherein ye were also careful, but ye lacked opportunity." Philippians 4:10.

72

Paul's appreciation of the kind gesture of the Philippians church teaches us some vital lessons.

1. Christian ministers should appreciate and commend the kind deeds of their members.

2. The best of God's children will experience the vicissitudes of life. He should therefore display godliness and contentment in whatever state he finds himself.

3. The Philippians church was committed and generous in giving. Even when the Apostle was not in their midst, they remembered to support his ministry.

4. Giving is an investment into the kingdom of God. It is laying up for us:

"...treasures in heaven, where neither moth nor rust doth corrupt, and where thieves do not break through nor steal." Matthew 6:20.

The believer who gives cheerfully, faithfully, consistently and bountifully is making a sure investment in the Kingdom. It is, however, pertinent to note that those who give to God as sinners or backsliders will reap no eternal profit.

5. Giving of our precious substance, money and time to cater to the needs of fellow believers is a spiritual service to God. Apostle Paul described it as "...an odour of a sweet smell, a sacrifice acceptable, well pleasing to God." (Philippians 4:18).

6. Leaders should earnestly pray for members of the church who graciously give their substance, time, money and entire lives for the propagation of the gospel. In response to their generosity, the Apostle prayed for them.

"My God shall supply all your need according to his riches in glory by Christ Jesus. Salute every saint in Christ Jesus...The grace of our Lord Jesus Christ be with you all. Amen." Philippians 4:19, 21-23.

Paul concluded this epistle by acknowledging the supporting role of his companions and conveying their greetings to the brethren. He also showered apostolic blessings and good wishes upon them. Salutation or greetings is a sign of courtesy or respect. Believers should learn to appreciate and commend ministerial companions. "...The brethren which are with me greet you." This reveals another sterling quality of leadership of the Apostle: he was a master team builder. Apart from the brethren which were with him, Apostle Paul also sent the greetings of "All the saints..."

However, I salute Senior Pastor Francis Banefe and members of the Regenerated Church of God in Nottingham for their prayers, love, cares and supports during my sickness. My humble appreciation also to Prophet Uebert Angel, a British-Zimbabwean charismatic evangelical preacher and the founder of Spirit Embassy, a Pentecostal Ministry in the United Kingdom for giving me the opportunity to minister and shared my testimonies in his church. I am very grateful to you sir. Moreover, many thanks to Reverends Michael and Mary Oluwakeye of Mountain Top Ministry in London for giving me the opportunity to minister and share my testimonies in their church. More anointing in Jesus name. Amen.

My further appreciation goes to Mr. Pitman Browne, a 'big offer' in the Afro-Caribbean community in Nottingham, for your honest encouragement and moral support during my sickness and during the production of this book. You are a brother indeed.

I would like to acknowledge my first daughter, Kerry, and my first son, Mark, who were always with me in the hospital and at home both day and night during my sickness. I am lucky to have you as children. Also, my profound expression of appreciation to all Pastors and members of churches in Nottingham, all social workers and the team of personal carers who have supported me at one time or another, my General Practitioner (GP), nurses, all hospital staff and the management of the City Hospital and Queen's Medical Centre in Nottingham, my friends both men and women who stood by me during my sickness. I would like to specially thank the staff and management of Break Barriers Nottingham for their meritorious high quality designed domiciliary care services provided to meet my needs in positive ways. The company worths my recommendation. Furthermore, I would like to thank the following people; Elaine Spare, Gary Foster, Sonia Foster for their kind help and assistance in enabling the production of this book and their commitment to Our Lord's work for the furtherance of the Gospel. Thank you all.

Finally, I would like to appreciate those who have taken time to read about the story of my healing testimony in this book. Surely God shall bless you as you spread the testimony to friends, family and throughout the world. Amen.